Rolling with Life's Punches

Rolling with Life's Punches

You CAN live life victoriously

by
Virginia Volk Thompson

Beacon Hill Press of Kansas City
Kansas City, Missouri

Unless otherwise designated, all Scripture quotations are taken from *The Holy Bible, New International Version* (NIV), copyright © 1973, 1978, 1984 by the International Bible Society.

KJV—King James Version.

10   9   8   7   6   5   4   3   2   1

I lovingly dedicate this book to friends who actively assist me in rolling with life's punches.

Maaike Thompson—my daughter
Naomi Hagood—my sister
Molly Pooley—my colleague
Judie Wilde—my prayer partner
Lois Malpass—my challenger
Linda Russell—my encourager
Beverly Martin—my secretary

Contents

Preface

The most urgent need in human living is to be able to roll with life's punches, to face life victoriously. Many people are living defeated and are inwardly beaten, thus outwardly ineffective. They lack the resources to live successfully. This book is addressed to that need.

Rolling with Life's Punches presents four areas of personal fulfillment that are essential to living a life of balance and productivity: Beginning with the physical needs, which are basic for survival, we move upward to the emotional, mental, and spiritual domains.

The social-minded must be patient, for the emphasis is on personal needs, upon which all human relationships depend. As the reader will see, all life is one, the inner and the outer being interdependent.

The privilege has been mine of presenting these concepts to postgraduate classes, to parenting groups, and to retreat participants. Many testify that they are now better equipped to roll with life's punches.

It is my prayer that many more will find through these pages a clear path from confused and defeated human living to living that is certain, creative, and victorious.

1

Life's Punches Are Inevitable

"Go, Lions! Sink that shot, sink that shot!" The high school gymnasium was filled to capacity. People stood in the doorways, the cheerleaders cheered, and the bands played. My eyes followed the green jersey with the gold number 24 on the back. The boy dribbled down the court and passed off to number 10, who shot the basketball through the hoop. Seconds later the buzzer sounded the end of the ball game. The crowd cheered wildly.

I was a proud mother. Our son, Roe, had thrown the pass that clinched the district basketball tournament. The following weekend we would travel to the southern end of the state where his team would compete for the state title.

As we drove south on the snow-packed freeway to attend those games, it wasn't the glories on the basketball court but thoughts of my upcoming surgery that consumed my attention. I considered all the possibilities and wondered how I would react if the outcome was more serious than anticipated. Could I face leaving the family and an enjoyable life? Could I cope with another woman sharing the life of my husband, Ernie, and possibly finishing raising our children?

These thoughts were depressing. This would be my fourth surgery in three years. I wasn't coping as well as before.

During my girlhood Dad had always declared, "You must learn to roll with the punches, Ginny. Life's punches are inevitable. So learn to roll with them. Otherwise life will be one big skid for you."

One big skid, that is how it was. And I had neither the ability nor the desire to roll with this one. Negative thoughts were in control during the 300-mile trip.

Inside the Minidome where the state tournament was about to begin, people were gathering and predicting that the green and gold Borah Lions would walk away with the state title.

The cold metal benches provided the seating area while waiting for the starting whistle. As the teams prepared for the game, the basketballs caught my attention: each ball as it was passed from player to player, bounced on the wooden floor, and tossed through the air at the basket. Sometimes it missed and bounced off the rim, or it rolled across the floor as the players chased it.

I took mental note of the characteristics of the basketball. It is round, filled to capacity, and has a strong outer surface. But what if the basketball was square? Or what if it had a flat side? What if it had a surface that was easily punctured?

A square basketball, a flat basketball, or a soft-surfaced basketball would be worthless. In order to play the game, the ball must be round, be filled with air, and have a tough outer surface.

Likewise, in order for one to roll with life's punches, he must have certain characteristics and specific qualities.

We were created by God to exhibit far greater versatility than a basketball. We are physical, emotional, mental, and spiritual beings. Because of these four distinct, yet interdependent, features, our potential is limitless. Yet in order to function effectively, we must be well-developed in all four areas.

It is important to inventory our present state of fitness to determine our health in each of these areas. We can then proceed to develop goals and methods to reach our full potential.

In spite of our circumstances, our environment, our background, our financial status, or our educational accomplishments, we can be the persons we were created to be, rolling with life's punches effectively, productively, and satisfactorily.

Life's punches come in many forms. Some are major, and we become temporarily incapacitated by them. Separation by death or divorce, suffering over long periods of time due to illness or accident, and financial reverses that seem overwhelming are among the worst.

During the past three years I have been hit, punched, and dribbled by many hurtful and prolonged circumstances and separations.

This series of punches began when word came that Father's health was failing rapidly and that he had a short time to live. Long periods of time were spent at his bedside, visiting with him about the joys of life, the certainty of death, and the expectations of heaven.

Each Saturday afternoon I drove 20 miles to be with him. Mother would brew a fresh pot of coffee and pour us a cup to sip while we visited. The little bell on their front doorknob would signal us that she had left to do some shopping. The television quietly mumbled in the background to reduce the weight of the silences that were interspersed with our conversations.

When Dad seemed tired and began to doze, I straightened his bed sheets, looked through his books, and read the jottings in his journal. His writings reassured me that, while his health was failing rapidly, he was continuing to face each day's joys and problems with courage, optimism, and hope. They evidenced that he was still looking for creative ways to solve his life's problems.

He wrote about his conflict with the home nurse, how to adjust his window blind from his bed, and named foods that irritated his digestive tract. He was continually seeking ways to improve relationships and to simplify his handicapped life-style.

While sitting in church one Sunday morning, I received a note from an usher that said Dad had died. Saturday afternoons would no longer be spent philosophizing with him.

This was a blessed time. Dad and I had talked it all out. We had shared life, shared death, and shared the hope of eternal life together. Knowing that he was not suffering made the loneliness more tolerable.

Following Dad's death, my appreciation for life was keener than before. Coffee smelled fresher, school bells sounded friendlier, hamburgers tasted better, and handshakes felt warmer. It seemed that after experiencing death, life offered more meaning. But one month later, Mother phoned, indicating she was entering the hospital for tests.

After the working day was finished, I anxiously hurried to the hospital. Mother had been the rock of our family. She was rarely sick.

"Mrs. Thompson," the nurse said, "your mother is in intensive care."

This was too great a shock for even an answer. But she's just here for tests, I thought.

It took several days for the test results to return. I waited, praying and exercising as much patience as could be mustered. But the results were not good: She had colon cancer.

First Dad, now Mother. The weeks and months that followed were filled with happy times. We did all of those things we loved so much—family dinners, rides in the country, shopping sprees, and long Sunday afternoon walks.

Mother did not allow the doctor's diagnosis to rob her of one morsel of the life she loved. She readjusted her social calendar and made sure that every friend was included. Some days she went to lunch three times in order to have equal time with everyone. It seemed that I was the one who needed an appointment to see her.

As the cancer began to disfigure her body, we wondered if she would withdraw from others and spend more time in seclusion. But her spunk was amazing. Like Dad, she faced each new circumstance with poise.

As we were shopping one afternoon, I said, "Mom, we might have to go to the maternity shop to get you a dress. They have beautiful clothes that would be more comfortable on you."

Matter-of-factly she smiled. "That's a great idea," she said, with not even a hint of self-pity.

Another time I asked her, "Mom, what is it like when you go to bed at night? It is dark, you are alone, and you know that you are going to die."

Again she smiled and said, "Ginny, I have had a good life. I have enjoyed it, and I know peace. I could die in a car accident before this cancer gets me."

I was being hit with life's punches, and she was teaching me to roll with them.

One afternoon we went to the high school track to exercise. As I jogged several times around the quarter mile, she walked only once and went to the car to rest. Each time I passed the car, she waved. Tears dripped down my cheeks and off my chin as her smile and her wave encouraged me to grasp all that life held—the good and the bad.

Even today I can see her smile and her wave when I

am running. They seem to say, "Ginny, life won't be easy. But embrace it. Accept it as a challenge. Keep on jogging."

This "jogging" included being at her bedside and holding her hand as she left me to run the race without a mother's cheers. Whatever loneliness I had experienced before was nothing compared to the realization that the ones who always understood and always cared were here no more.

The final blow to my stability came as a surprise. The morning was uneventful at school while teaching 24 smiling fourth graders. But just before noon, our son Roe, who was 25 years old, walked into the classroom and sat quietly at the back. I finished teaching math and took the students to the lunchroom. When I returned to the classroom, Roe was staring at the floor.

"Hi, son. What brings you here?"

"Nothing good."

"What do you mean?"

"Mom, I went to see Dr. Walker this morning. He is 99 percent sure I have a malignant tumor. He wants to operate tomorrow."

Neither of us said anything for a few minutes.

Finally Roe broke the silence. "Mom, how are you going to handle this?"

I didn't know. There followed a search for words to express optimism, but they wouldn't come.

After a long moment I said, "Son, we will see it through together. We will not give up. We will fight it to the finish."

He hugged me. "Thanks, Mom," he said. "I needed to hear you say that."

Tears welled up in my eyes as I watched him walk slowly out of the classroom, down the long school hallway, and out the door into the chill of the day. His shoulders were stooped, and my heart was filled with fears.

The next day Ernie went with Roe to the hospital. The operation confirmed that the tumor was malignant, and the radiation treatments were scheduled.

During his radiation treatments, Roe was often too sick to be alone. He would phone me to come and get him. I would take him home, tuck him into bed, rub his back, and silently pray until he fell asleep.

All of life's punches aren't that severe, but they are every bit as irritating: trying to sleep while the neighbor's dog barks on and on and on; facing a job for which you have no motivation, no appreciation, no desire; your car stalling on the freeway; oversleeping on the morning you face the most promising opportunity of your life.

All of these are punches. How we deal with them depends on how well-rounded we are physically, emotionally, mentally, and spiritually.

WHERE ARE YOU BEING HIT?

Before we can equip ourselves to roll, we must determine the nature of our punches. It is the little nagging ones that usually cause us to skid.

Find a quiet place where you can be alone and reflect over the past week. What problems, trials, or irritating situations have you encountered? List them on the lines below. Be specific, for a vague problem will not have a clear-cut solution.

PROBLEM	NO.	REACTION

Determine approximately how many times you have been hit with the same problem this week. Write the number in the small square. Finally, write your reaction to each situation in the space provided.

"Search me, O God, and know my heart; test me and know my anxious thoughts" (Ps. 139:23).

2

Only the Well-rounded Roll

A regulation-size basketball is required for official game play and is also used for practice sessions. While our children scrimmage on the driveway with a red, white, and blue basketball, a game ball is brown leather and has OFFICIAL written boldly on the side.

Likewise, if we are to roll properly through life, God has some official requirements for us. He set these in motion when man was created, and they have to do with developing and maintaining each aspect of our personality.

Physical well-roundedness is the discipline to provide for our bodies the essential ingredients for optimum performance.

Weeks, months, and several years of suffering with long periods of chemical imbalances were finally ended by the diagnosis that I had a life-style ailment. In the attempt to be superwoman, I had spent years concentrating on the needs of others but ignoring my own physical needs.

This problem was not one that could be solved by surgery or medication. It had to be solved personally. I had to understand what my needs were and then be willing to alter my life-style.

I learned to become aware of my body and how it reacts to foods, activities, and stresses. I read widely on the subject of life-style health and enrolled in classes on nutrition and stress management. Essentially, I accepted the responsibility to ensure a life of physical well-roundedness.

Emotional well-roundedness is evidenced in our relationships. When we learn not to place blame on others, on ourselves, or on our environment, we are in good emotional health. Most of us know people who always seem to need someone to blame. It seems that the threat of failure or criticism causes them to look for an escape immediately.

A teaching colleague could not admit making even an insignificant mistake. On one occasion she checked some books out of the school district library; but when the due date came, she couldn't find them. The librarian began calling to request the books. The teacher responded to the calls by saying, "I sent them back. They must have been lost in the mail." The mystery of the lost books was unsolved for many weeks.

One day while cleaning a storage closet, I came across the lost books and told the teacher that the books were found. Without saying a word to anyone, she mailed the books and acted as if she had never found them. Her silence in the matter continued to displace blame. Her ability to roll with the punches was hampered by her fear to admit a mistake.

Mental well-roundedness is the ability to be challenged and not defeated by life's situations.

The diagnosis of Mother's cancer did not defeat her. It challenged her. She chose to look at the positive instead of dwelling on the negative. She learned everything she could about her particular kind of cancer so that she could make wise choices concerning her care. She gave up those things that seemed unnecessary and concentrated on the important matters. Relationships were more important to her than money. Thus, she gave her checkbook to my sister. She didn't want to be bothered with dollars; she wanted to be involved with people.

This mental attitude toward a difficult situation illustrates mental well-roundedness.

Spiritual well-roundedness is an inner awareness and a peace that assures us we are in harmony with our Creator.

During those weeks that Dad lay in bed, knowing that his life was slowly ebbing from him, he evidenced spiritual well-roundedness. He expressed satisfaction in the values he had adopted early in life and had adhered to throughout the years. While his bodily functions were failing, he had an inner calm that assured us he was at peace with the God of the universe. He spoke freely of his coming death and admonished me to establish habits and values that I not only could live by but also would be comfortable with when facing death.

"Ginny," he said one afternoon, "I feel like I am floating on billows of white, fluffy clouds. It reminds me of looking out an airplane window at a sea of clouds and realizing I am engulfed in them. I am relaxed and at peace."

I could see the oxygen tubes in his nose and hear his labored breathing. But he was no longer aware of life's distractions. Spiritually, he was in good health.

To maintain well-roundedness in each of the four areas we've discussed, it's important to have balanced input and output. Physical input includes diet, exercise, and rest. Physical output is manifested in what we accomplish with our bodies through work and recreation.

When there is more input than output in body, mind, or spirit, stagnation and fat develop, and efficiency and productivity decrease.

Likewise, when we are giving out more than we are taking in, our system malfunctions, and we become burned out, fatigued, and without resources.

Emotional input includes affirming oneself, reaching one's goals, and experiencing positive relationships. Emotional output is sharing our positive feelings with others.

A good activity for your emotional health is to make a list of all the things you do well. Mine reads something like this:

I am honest.
I am fun.
I am a good friend.
I am an inspired and motivated teacher.
I am a good organizer.
I am a good runner.

This is an affirmation list. Too often we are aware of only the things we don't do as effectively as we would like. As a result, our own negative thoughts hamper us emotionally.

We may tend to set goals when we are depressed in an effort to offset our feelings of failure. Setting realistic goals and reaching them is important to the emotionally well-rounded individual.

When our boys were in high school, they played interscholastic sports. The day after a poor performance I would often find a new list of goals in their rooms.

—run 5 miles every day
—100 sit-ups
—50 push-ups
—45 minutes on weights
—2 hours team practice

Their goals were unrealistic and unattainable. As a result, they failed physically and were defeated emotionally as well.

Goal setting is more profitable when the goals are established at a time when we can be objective and realistic concerning our time and potential.

Another barometer of our emotional health is found in our relationships. While we do not have control over all

24

relationships, we can maintain emotional balance by making sure our part of the relationship is free of bitterness, resentment, anger or blame. Conflict in any relationship is inevitable and has many faces and forms.

I recently had a conflict with the building principal. I was upset by his actions and hurt over what seemed a lack of confidence in my ability to handle a student. My emotional state stabilized only after I forgave him. During the time I held onto the misunderstanding, I was not free. I didn't want to face him in the hallway or say, "Good morning," at the front door. I was my own worst enemy when it came to rolling with the punches of a normal school day.

Mental input includes everything that goes into our minds through our five senses. And mental output is demonstrated through our thoughts and ideas, our spoken and written words.

Our minds have an amazing capacity to perceive and process the vast amount of information and feelings we experience daily. We are continually exposed to conflicting input, and each experience is processed and stored within our conscious or subconscious memory. Our productivity and efficiency largely depend on what is stored within the confines of our mind. While we cannot control every influence that affects our minds, we can choose to think upon those things that will stimulate mental well-roundedness.

Fear is one of the destructive influences on the mind. It doesn't matter how insignificant the fear may seem to others. If it is allowed to linger on the mind's screen too long, it will cause crippling effects on our entire being.

I have a fear of traveling on slick roads. One Christmas we were traveling to another state, and the first half of our trip was blessed with sunshine and dry roads. During this time I felt wonderful. I visited freely with Ernie and the children, read a book, and listened joyously to the music on the radio.

As afternoon approached, the clouds hid the sun, and the pavement was damp. I began to fear when only two dry tire paths were left. My eyes became glued to these dry spots and the amount of snowpack in between them. When the snowpack spread clear across the freeway, and no dry spots were evident, I panicked. I stopped visiting, put away the book, and turned off the radio. My body felt rigid, as I did nothing but watch the road. I'd lost the ability to roll with the punch and mentally was in an uncontrollable skid. Eventually I realized what was happening. I found my journal and began to write a list of the times we had traveled on slick roads in the past, then visualized each time we had safely arrived at our destination without accident or harm. I convinced myself that Ernie had evidenced the skills to meet all prior emergencies and that he still had the capacity to use these skills. On my mind's screen, I flashed successes instead of possible failures.

While my mental skidding didn't completely stop until we arrived safely, the day was sufficiently tolerable because I changed my mental focus from failure to success.

Spiritual input for me includes Bible reading, prayer, and meditation. The output is loving, caring, and sharing with others.

Again, Dad illustrates the complete cycle of the spiritually well-rounded. During his mid-20s Dad realized a link was missing in his life. He was not experiencing the fulfillment and joy that he believed was available.

He did not find the fulfillment he longed for in his occupation, his family, or his activities. As his search continued, he realized those who evidenced peace in the good times and in the bad times had one ingredient in common: They had an avenue of spiritual input and expression.

26

His search continued. There are many forms of spiritual expression, with each providing a source of meaning and purpose to converts. Dad listened to people of various persuasions and read the origins of many religions.

When Dad understood the gospel of Jesus Christ, he found the element missing in his life. His quest did not end at salvation; he continued to search the Scriptures, and discovery became a daily event in his life. This element of discovering new truths, plus the vital relationship he was developing with the person of Jesus Christ, provided him with a spiritual stamina that not only equipped him to roll with life's punches but also provided a continual flow of spiritual vitality to those around him. No wonder he faced death with confidence and assurance years later.

Heather and I sat across the table from each other as she shared: "I am ready for the loony bin. I have seen a dozen doctors and still don't have an answer. I don't know where to turn, but I am losing my mind.

"My back aches. I can't sleep. I'm dizzy, and I have blinding headaches. I explode over every irritation, and I have no motivation."

Some of the punches Heather was experiencing were three teenage sons and a teenage daughter who were having difficulty finding their way through the growing-up jungle. Besides her children's problems, Heather was attempting to do her part in putting a marriage back together that had terminated after 20 miserable years. She had been separated from her husband for one year and was now trying to rekindle love, harmony, and satisfaction in their marriage. Heather also had a demanding job that required her to work long hours with dangerous equipment and do some heavy lifting.

Heather's output far exceeded her input. While she was giving a great deal to others, she had not made it a priority to fill herself. Now she was empty, and there was nothing left to give. Her body, mind, and spirit were dry and useless.

Even though Heather's vessel was empty, she had hope. Heather had clearly defined her symptoms, which is step one in regaining health. Second, she was being honest with herself and with others about her condition. She was not masking the reality of her plight, hoping that no one would notice. And, third, Heather was actively seeking help. But the ingredient that most likely assured her recovery was her willingness to act on the advice she was given.

Little by little Heather began to plan into her day specific activities that provided nourishment physically, emotionally, mentally, and spiritually.

For physical renewal Heather took a 10-minute walk each day. The exercise stimulated blood circulation and provided fresh oxygen. She also added fresh fruits and vegetables to her diet on a regular basis. And she learned to turn off the TV at a reasonable hour to get needed rest.

Heather planned 10 minutes into her day to improve her emotional state. She chose to accomplish one task from beginning to end each day for a feeling of worth and fulfillment. As she completed each task, her emotional health was improved.

Heather set aside a third 10-minute period in her day for mental stimulation. She asked questions, sought answers, and stretched her mind into creative, problem-solving sessions.

Spiritually, she analyzed her value system and began her search for spiritual expression by reading books, asking questions, and listening to various authorities. She also planned quiet times of meditation, which brought about some immediate relief and release. She set aside 10 minutes of her day for this spiritual reflection and found that it strengthened her ability to face each day with peace and poise.

As Heather's personality became more rounded, she began to roll with the punches effectively.

ARE YOU EQUIPPING YOURSELF TO ROLL?

Drill 1: Physically

List your favorite foods.

1. _____   6. _____

2. _____   7. _____

3. _____   8. _____

4. _____   9. _____

5. _____   10. _____

Draw a line through the foods on your list that are high in refined sugar, fat, and salt.

List your favorite exercises.

1. _____   3. _____

2. _____   4. _____

Draw a line through the ones you haven't done this week.

Write the number of hours of sleep you have had each night this week.

Mon. _____   Tues. _____   Wed. _____

Thurs. _____   Fri. _____   Sat. _____   Sun. _____

Draw a line through the nights you didn't have adequate sleep for your personal needs.

Drill 2: Emotionally

What is something you do well? _____

_____

What is something you want to do better? _____

_____

What three words (qualities) would you like people to associate with you?

_____ , _____ , _____

With whom do you have a satisfying relationship? __

_____

How do you contribute to its satisfaction? _____

_____

_____

With whom do you have an unsatisfactory relationship?

_____

How do you contribute to its dissatisfaction? _____

_____

_____

Drill 3: Mentally

List your five favorite books.

_____

_____

_____

_____

_____

What book are you now reading?

_____

How many minutes do you read each week?

_____

List your five favorite TV programs.

_____

_____

_____

_____

_____

How many minutes do you watch TV each week?

_____

Who is your mental stretcher?

_____

When did you last have contact with that person?

_____

How many quiet minutes do you spend to problem
solve or to dream each week?

_____

Drill 4: Spiritually

What one belief is evidenced by your life-style in all
situations?

_____

What do you believe is your purpose in life? _____

_____

What belief or beliefs do you wish to pass on to others?

_____

_____

_____

_____

_____

Who has been most influential in developing your present beliefs? _____

_____

Who is being influenced most by your beliefs? _____

_____

_____

"A man reaps what he sows" (Gal. 6:7)—physically, emotionally, mentally, and spiritually.

3

Physical Well-roundedness

To win a basketball game takes teamwork. And to attain physical well-roundedness, the parts of our body must work together as a team.

It was a Monday morning when I arrived in Portland, Oreg. A friend picked me up at the airport and drove across town to the University of Oregon Medical School Hospital. After a lengthy check-in I was assigned to room 321 and put to bed.

Before long a doctor appeared and began asking questions.

"How do you feel?"

"I am weak. I feel like I've been turned upside down, and all of the strength has been poured out."

"Do you feel this way at any particular time of the day?"

"I feel this way all the time. I can hardly put one foot in front of the other."

"Do you have any other symptoms?"

"I am light-headed, dizzy, and short of breath. My fingers, arms, and legs tingle and are numb. I also find it difficult to concentrate. My thoughts are goofy."

He asked other routine questions, closed his writing book, and bid me good-day.

Shortly, a second doctor came in, introduced himself,

sat down, and began to ask the same questions. After he left, the questioning was repeated by five more doctors.

I finally asked the seventh doctor why so many doctors came to see me and why they all asked the same questions.

He explained they were a team, and their task was to diagnose my illness. By each of them doing his own questioning, there was a higher probability that they could gather needed information. What one doctor missed, another one might catch. Also, I might be able to shed more light on the problem while continuing the talking.

At that point in life I was sick in body. I functioned at about 25 percent capacity and was searching for answers.

The answers to these health problems did not materialize on that trip to Portland, nor did I find them during the second time in that same hospital. But slowly the pieces to the puzzle were uncovered. Bit by bit I discovered that my poor health was due to life-style. If I wanted to be well, the approach to life had to change. Attitudes needed changing. Eating habits, exercise patterns, and sleep habits all had to change. I was my own worst enemy.

Say the word "fitness," and you will surely get a reaction. Recently several friends came over for a summer brunch. Our conversation was light and pleasant until someone brought up the subject of physical fitness. Each person at the table had a definite opinion about the topic.

Bonnie praises swimming laps. Billie swears by water aerobics. Lorraine believes that cycling is best. May insists the only sensible exercise is walking. I chose not to express an opinion. But Shirley finally spoke up and said that the entire fitness movement is insane. She likes to eat ice cream dripping with hot fudge and has no desire to look like a model.

At 45 years of age, my 5 feet 4 inches frame weighed 165 pounds. For many years I had determined that at the time of becoming a little old lady, I wanted to be a jogger. Then came the realization that I was almost a little old lady and had better start jogging. But the thought of running down the block out of breath, and sweating, was depressing.

Hope came through the words of former Miss America Marilyn VandeBur. During one of her motivational lectures, she looked straight at me and said, "You, too, can do it. If you set a goal, develop a plan, and work hard, you can reach your potential, your dream."

It clicked! I knew it could be done. Physical fitness was within reach.

I began a walk/jog program. At first it was mostly walk. Soon I could actually jog one mile. And for a year I jogged a mile a day. I hated every step but stayed with it.

A colleague challenged me to run in a two-mile fun run. When I did, it was a major event for the family as well. Ernie took movies just as he does for the children's sport events. Everyone was proud of Mom, and it was good to know I, too, had physical strength.

Shortly thereafter I read *Fit or Fat,* by Covert Bailey. It was another challenge. There was not only a need to exercise but also a need to rid my body of its fat. My entire life-style needed to be changed. The goal: wellness, good health.

Ernie and I enrolled in a high-level health program. A doctor tested us to determine our level of fitness. Blood tests revealed cholesterol levels as well as other pertinent information. They checked our body fat, flexibility, and endurance. We also took a written exam to determine life-style habits and stressors.

Following our fitness profile, we began a series of classes emphasizing that each of us has personal responsibility for our health. We were encouraged to work on only one area of change at a time.

My first change was to eliminate fat in the diet. Cheese, eggs, butter, and other fat sources were cut out.

Breakfast has now progressed from omelets to whole grain cereal, fruit, and skim milk. A normal lunch consists of a vegetable salad, chicken or fish, and occasionally a bran muffin. And dinner is long on fruits, vegetables, and lean meat, with little emphasis on desserts.

I also chose the exercise that was most enjoyable and that could fit into the schedule the easiest: jogging.

The third phase of this physical well-roundedness program was to consider stress factors. I had to learn to say no to commitments that overloaded the schedule.

Saying no is difficult for some of us. Preplanning was my key to success in this area. If I have previously determined to have only two commitments per month, outside home and job, it is easier to say, "I am sorry. I am already committed to another task"; or "I will have to drop another commitment if I accept this one."

Ernie and I also began to check each other's calendar so that we don't have conflicting commitments. We find that respecting each other's priorities, and not over-committing, has cut down on the stress between us. And job-related stresses are more manageable when we have a minimum of stress at home.

A remarkable stress reliever has been to plan ahead and be early.

I used to calculate exactly how long it would take to do the grocery shopping. If that was one hour, I would promise Ernie to return in an hour. What these calculations failed to consider were the slow drivers and full check-out lines. Thus our stress levels increased with every minute I was detained beyond the hour. My head started aching, and my attitude deteriorated.

Now I calculate how long it might take to shop, and

double it. If there are a few spare minutes, I indulge in window shopping or having a frozen yogurt.

This time doubling has also been a great stress reliever for arriving at appointments composed and on time. If the need is to leave at 6:30 to arrive by 6:45, I plan to leave at 6:15.

The fourth factor in physical well-roundedness is rest. We can greatly benefit from learning our limits and understanding the point where we are no longer productive because our bodies are so fatigued.

When we adults are tired, no one will tell us to go to bed. It is our responsibility to know when we need rest. When we are tired, we should tell our family, ask them to be quiet, and go to bed. It was amazing to discover that I had not only the right to be tired and go to bed but also the full support of the family. They really cared, and they protected me from interruptions.

Physical well-roundedness is essential if we are to roll with life's punches. But each of us must determine what we need to develop and maintain physical health and vitality.

PHYSICAL PLAN

Drill 1: Diet

> Develop a one-week plan to improve your physical condition.

MEALS

	BREAKFAST	LUNCH	DINNER
SUNDAY			
MONDAY			
TUESDAY			
WEDNESDAY			
THURSDAY			
FRIDAY			
SATURDAY			

Prepare your shopping list for the week's meals.

_____   _____   _____

_____   _____   _____

_____   _____   _____

_____   _____   _____

_____   _____   _____

Drill 2: Exercise

Type _____

Duration _____

Drill 3: Rest

To bed at _____; up at _____

Drill 4: Evaluation

At the end of the week write a summary of how you
feel physically and how that affects your ability to roll.

_____

_____

_____

_____

_____

_____

_____

_____

"Therefore, I urge you, brothers, in view of God's mercy, to
offer your bodies as living sacrifices, holy and pleasing to
God" (Rom. 12:1).

4

Emotional Well-roundedness

Even though the official basketball is in perfect condition, it does not always go through the hoop when it is shot. An offensive rebound is necessary, or a trip down to the other end of the court and back. Similarly, we need not become emotional wrecks every time our effort to score is checked.

I am a giver. This means I am sensitive to the needs of others and will make great personal sacrifices for them.

As a giver, I have often experienced unnecessary emotional stresses because it is difficult to express personal preferences and needs.

This year Saturday mornings were scheduled for writing time. I wanted to sleep until rested, go for a run, shower, eat, and then spend three to four hours writing. The first three Saturdays were terrific. Then the interruptions began, and the emotional stress built.

Robert brought a friend to breakfast. Ernie wanted me to pick up the lawn mower at the repair shop. I was asked to speak at a ladies' brunch. Soon writing on Saturday mornings had been crowded completely out of the schedule.

I did not tell Robert his friend could come to breakfast Sunday but not Saturday. I did not tell Ernie I couldn't pick up the mower until later in the day. And I did not tell the ladies I was unavailable on Saturday mornings.

41

This inner conflict that led to such emotional trauma happened for various reasons. For one thing I simply could not say no or express inner wants. Everyone else took priority. Another reason was the highly idealistic goal that was set of blocking off what in many households is often a busy time of the week, and then brooking no interruptions. Then again, I didn't consider that as a child of God, He has the right to rearrange my schedule. After all, it is a privilege to serve a son and his friend, help a husband, and especially minister to a group of ladies who wanted me to speak to them.

I like being a giver and choose it freely over the other extreme: being a taker. However, my emotional balance is easily disturbed by carrying my problems plus everyone else's. No matter what the conflict or the reason for it, I tend to say, "I'm sorry." I have taken blame even when the conflict was between our children or colleagues. As a result, I can quickly lose self-respect, thinking I must be really bad or all this conflict would not be going on.

An example of internalizing blame happened while lunching with Lois. While we were standing at the hostess station, waiting to be seated, an elderly lady started walking toward us. About eight feet in front of us, she stumbled and nearly fell. I lunged to catch her and said, "Oh, I'm sorry."

Lois responded, "Why are you sorry? You didn't do anything." I suddenly realized that I had internalized a happening and owned blame for a near accident that I had no part in.

Thomas Gordon shed the healing light upon my emotional being in his book *Parent Effectiveness Training.* His theory is that in a conflict situation, the one who is upset owns the problem; the only time a problem becomes ours, he wrote, is when we become upset.

Free at last! The following week I was leading my students to the lunchroom at noon when another teacher and her class came down the hallway out of turn. The teacher said, "Oh, I guess we are early," to which I calmly replied, "Yes, you are."

My response normally would have been, "Oh, that's all right. You go ahead. We will wait."

My colleague couldn't look me in the eye or talk to me for almost a week. Several times I was tempted to own the problem and say, "I'm sorry." But I chose to allow her ownership of her feelings. Communication was restored without confrontation.

Emotional damage also occurs when our feelings lead us to believe that we have no value.

I have taught school with Molly for 18 years. Whether she is teaching, or camping, Molly dresses perfectly for the occasion. She's one of those stunning women other women don't like to see.

One spring morning I came to school in a new dress, feeling especially good about the way I looked—until I saw Molly, who looked better.

What had started out as a good morning suddenly crumbled into awfulness. It seemed that no matter how I looked, Molly always looked better. I was criticizing my appearance, and more importantly, my self-worth.

However, my self-image was not Molly's problem; it was mine. I had to own it and accept the responsibility for a change of attitude. I made a list of my good qualities, such as being a creative teacher, well organized, sensing the needs of others, and taking time to listen to them. When Molly returned to the room, I complimented her on her appearance and also made a positive comment about myself.

Another step to emotional well-roundedness is to train ourselves to see the good. It is an excellent habit to start each day with words of affirmation.

As you look at yourself in the mirror, practice saying three positive things to yourself:

> I am an honest person.
> I worked hard yesterday.
> I look really good today.

At the breakfast table say three positive things to family members:

> I appreciate your getting home on time last night.
> Thanks for filling my car with gas.
> You sent a great lunch with me yesterday.

Next, say three positive things about the day:

> I am glad I have a job.
> The neighbor's new car is really pretty.
> I enjoy the green hills and the blue sky.

Say three positive things to God:
"Thank You for food, for health, and for someone to love."

Being positive is a choice each of us makes. No one can force us to be negative if we choose to be positive. And when we feel good about ourselves and others, our emotions help us to roll with the punches.

> *Two men looked out from prison bars.*
> *One saw mud, the other stars.*
> —Unknown

Being positive is seeing stars when you could see mud. It means believing the best about others and admiring their attributes without jealousy.

The March afternoon was perfect for running. The temperature was 60 degrees, and only a slight breeze blew against our faces. This was our first time to run together, but rapport between us was readily established. We kept the same pace comfortably.

Zoe Ann's petite body was tanned a deep bronze. Her black ponytail swished with each step. Her turquoise shorts matched her shirt and her Nike socks.

I observed her confident manner and smiled at the contrast. She was 28; I was 48. My body was still winter white. My sweatpants were a dull gray and my cotton shirt a bright orange that clashed with my lavender running shoes.

The first mile we ran in silence.

"I am writing a new book," I said finally.

"What about?" she asked.

"It's called 'Rolling with Life's Punches.'"

"What do you mean by that?"

I outlined the book ideas and concluded: "If we put the right ingredients into our day, we can experience fulfillment and joy even in adverse situations."

"What do you do, Ginny? You are so relaxed. I know your life has been difficult recently. What ingredients do you put into your life in order to live this way?"

"For my physical health I eat meals that supply me with energy, I exercise, and I get adequate sleep. For my emotional well-being I nurture at least one relationship daily, and I forgive my offenders quickly. To maintain my mental alertness, I stretch my mind with new ideas and concepts. I also guard my mind from negative influences. And for my spiritual vitality, I spend time each day reading my Bible, meditating on wholesome issues, and praying for God's will to be accomplished in my life."

"That must take a lot of time," she mused.

"No. It saves me time because my productivity and efficiency levels are raised to optimum. I accomplish more and do it with ease."

Silence settled in once more. The only sounds were an occasional car, a barking dog, and the pounding of our feet on the blacktop.

When we had accomplished our five-mile run, we sat our sweaty bodies down to drink a Diet Coke. I looked at Zoe Ann. I wasn't sure if it was a tear or perspiration on her cheek. I said nothing.

It was a tear. That tear was followed by a flood of tears. "Ginny, I have to tell someone. I am dying inside.

"I'm bulimic. For nine years I have regurgitated everything I have eaten. I can't even look at myself in the mirror. I am so ugly."

I was stunned. Zoe Ann was so well kept on the outside and yet so neglected on the inside. How could a girl be so beautiful to others and yet so ugly to herself?

Through her sobs, Zoe Ann asked if I thought applying the concepts in "Rolling with Life's Punches" would help her.

Together we designed a program to roll instead of skid. But we also began to nurture a relationship. I became her sounding board; she became a means for me to share the concepts God was teaching me. Thus a mutual nurturing, which was health-producing for us both, was born.

Zoe Ann joined Overeaters Anonymous, where she found caring assistance. The regular meetings helped her regain her now healthy life-style.

The most important factor in emotional well-roundedness is in the full realization that we have great value in the mind of God. He knew each of us while we were being formed in our mother's womb. He planned all the days of our lives. Each morning when we awake, His thoughts are on us.

There are times when it seems no one understands. Our ability to maintain emotional health depends upon our knowing that God loves us just as we are.

EMOTIONAL PLAN

Drill 1: Accomplishments

Make a list of the tasks you need to do that could be completed in 10 minutes.

_____   _____

_____   _____

_____   _____

_____   _____

_____   _____

For one week choose one task each day and complete it.

Drill 2: Self-affirmations

Complete the following sentences:

I like myself for _____.

I enjoy myself when _____.

I please myself when _____.

I applaud myself for _____.

I am proud of myself for _____.

I laugh with myself when _____.

I admire myself for _____.

Read your self-affirmations each morning for one week.

47

Drill 3: Relationships

Make a list of people with whom you would like to get acquainted.

_____

_____

_____

_____

Plan a specific time this week to touch the life of one person. It may be a note, a phone call, lunch, or a walk in the park.

Make a list of people with whom you have a strained relationship.

_____

_____

_____

_____

_____

Forgive them in your heart and mind, and in person if you feel it is necessary.

Drill 4: Evaluation

At the end of the week write a summary of how you feel emotionally and how that affects your ability to roll.

_____

_____

_____

_____

_____

_____

_____

_____

_____

"Don't you know that you yourselves are God's temple and that God's Spirit lives in you? If anyone destroys God's temple, God will destroy him" (1 Cor. 3:16).

"Each of you should look not only to your own interests, but also to the interests of others" (Phil. 2:4).

5

Mental Well-roundedness

Benny Arnold lived to be 45, but his mind did not develop beyond that of a 10-year-old. During my childhood years, Benny often ran away from his home and came to visit us. I was too young to understand what made him different, but I developed a sensitivity to his need and to his limitations.

On one of his unannounced visits I was home with my older sister and brother, who were both disturbed and amused by his arrival. They were old enough to realize that Benny's presence could result in any number of unpleasant situations.

In their attempt to ensure calm, they brought out the Monopoly game for all of us to play. They were uneasy when I sat on the couch and held Benny's hand instead of playing the game.

After a couple of tense hours, our parents returned and calmly led Benny back to his home. My sister still teases me about sitting on the couch, holding hands with Benny Arnold.

Benny was not responsible for his mental limitations, and his inabilities made me sad. Even more disheartening is knowing that people I live, work, and play with are making daily choices to destroy their minds.

Connie was 40 years old when she gave birth to Beth,

her youngest child. She was most unhappy about this intrusion. Her two older children were becoming self-sufficient, and Connie did not want to start over with a new baby.

She allowed her anger to turn inward, causing resentment, depression, and an assortment of physical ailments. Her doctor prescribed Valium and Librium to alter her mood swings instead of helping her face the root of her problem.

Every few months she returned to the doctor with an increasing number of symptoms—obesity, high blood pressure, sweats, and headaches. The doctor prescribed greater doses of Valium and Librium to keep her in control.

Connie's family was the target for her outbursts of anger. Her explosions were followed by more medication and a dulling of her senses.

Through her choices and her doctor's assistance, Connie was destroying her mind and her body. Her ability to live a productive life was slipping from her grasp, and she found herself on a downhill skid with nothing in sight to stop her.

Eventually her husband intervened. "Connie, you have a drug problem," he told her. "You are addicted, and I am taking you to the care unit."

She later told me that the confrontation with her husband brought great relief. She found that she had a support system at home and at work. She had doctors and nurses who could teach her how to cope with her anger without chemicals. Today Connie is making choices to use her mind instead of abusing it. She is also nurturing a relationship with her daughter.

According to psychologists Minirth and Meier, we have the power to choose whether we maintain a healthy mind or a depressed mind. In their book *Happiness Is a Choice,* they write: "All human beings are capable of inner joy and peace if they will choose it and follow the path to obtain it."

Our choices directly affect our state of mind. Ultimately we are a product of the choices we make.

Lisa and I were close friends when our children were small. We often had coffee together and shared books or recipes. But our lives drifted apart when we began to make different choices. She became engulfed in steamy romance novels, TV serials, drinking beer, and the man next door. Meanwhile, I enrolled in adult education classes and read books.

Lisa moved to another city, and I lost track of her. For 10 years I didn't hear from her.

Recently she came to Boise and phoned me, and we went to dinner. The contrast in our lives is staggering. She has experienced brokenness in the worst sense. She has no family, no job, and few possessions. Worst of all, she has no hope. She allowed her mind to dwell on things that are not pure, lovely, honest, or righteous. And she has become a slave to thoughts and habits that have robbed her of happiness.

The human mind is a great storehouse of information, sorting every impulse of sight, sound, smell, touch, and taste. We must control what we store inside. Each of us has the right to choose what we allow to be stored in our mind. And we become a living product of what we feed it.

Our ability to think and to choose what we think can fortify us with a plan before we meet temptations.

Lea was climbing out of the pit of alcoholism. I encouraged her to use the resources of her mind to predetermine what she would do in certain situations.

At five o'clock, when the rest of the office staff went for a cocktail, she didn't have to stammer or stutter an excuse, for she had planned alternatives. She chose to prearrange engagements and appointments.

On the nights that Lea knew she would be experiencing loneliness, she enrolled in an adult education class. She learned to think ahead, to think creatively, before facing the question of "to drink or not to drink." If we are to roll with life's punches, we must take control of our minds instead of being victimized by them.

Another aspect of being mentally fit is having someone to challenge us. "Mental stretchers" are people who teach us to think creatively and productively.

Dr. Jarrell Garsee was our pastor for 10 years. During this time he was my mental stretcher. He developed ideas that challenged me to think, and opened up what seemed to be limitless possibilities for application.

Often, while pondering a concept, I phoned Dr. Garsee for his opinion. He did not give opinions, though; he responded to questions with more questions. He forced me to come to my own conclusions.

During our early years of parenting, my friend Velda was my mental stretcher.

Roe was just finishing the first grade when he started lying, cheating, and stealing. We received daily phone calls from his teacher, telling of his unacceptable behavior. I had to take him to the manager of the grocery store to return stolen marbles and gum. Finally, he came down with the chicken pox. His rush of activities was curtailed for a few days, which provided time to think.

In desperation I phoned Velda, who said, "I think Roe is having to endure something that is too much for his little mind to cope with. Has he told you how he feels about school?"

He hadn't. This was the clue. My first question was, "Roe, do you like your teacher?"

He burst into tears and sobbed, "No, I hate her." We found out Roe had good reasons for the way he felt. We

54

kept him home the remaining two weeks of the year, and we didn't have a recurrence of the problems.

Velda didn't tell me what to do, but she provided a vehicle upon which my mind could arrive at the root of Roe's problem.

Each of us needs an intellectual stretcher, someone who challenges us to think new thoughts. Stretchers are often authors, speakers, teachers, or ministers who have the ability to lead us to the threshold of our own minds to make decisions of our own.

Many people do not know what they really believe. They only know what Dr. Dobson, Chuck Swindoll, or Ann Kiemel Anderson believes.

When life gives us one of those hard punches, it isn't very important what someone else thinks. But it is vital what we think. For our own problem-solving abilities are our only source of rolling with the punches of life.

MENTAL PLAN

Drill 1: Interests

Make a list of topics that interest you, or ones that you desire to know more about.

_____

_____

_____

_____

Find one book and one magazine article that relates to your interests. Read 10 minutes each day for one week.

Make a list of people you know who are knowledgeable about your interests.

_____

_____

_____

Telephone, write a letter, or make an appointment to discuss the topic with an expert.

Drill 2: Choose to Problem Solve

Choose one TV program that you will give up this week, and use the time creatively to solve a problem you have.

Define the problem.

_____

_____

_____

List possible solutions.

_____

_____

_____

List possible consequences of each solution.

_____

_____

_____

Choose a solution. Make a decision. Evaluate your decision at a later date to determine if you would choose the same solution another time.

Drill 3: Worries

List every concern or worry that you now have under MY OWN WORRIES. Place a check in the appropriate column determining whether or not you can do anything about each worry. Make a TO DO LIST for the worries that you can do something about.

MY OWN WORRIES	CAN	CAN'T	TO DO LIST
1.			
2.			
3.			
4.			
5.			
6.			

Drill 4: Evaluate

At the end of the week write a summary of how you were stimulated mentally and how that affected your ability to roll.

_____

_____

_____

_____

_____

"Whatever is true, whatever is noble, whatever is right, whatever is pure, whatever is lovely, whatever is admirable—if anything is excellent or praiseworthy—think about such things" (Phil. 4:8).

6

Spiritual Well-roundedness

In game play, the basketball is shifted from offensive players to the defensive ones without the slightest warning. We, too, can be functioning effectively and suddenly be jolted by an unexpected bounce.

I was a senior in high school when Ernie asked me for our first date. We went to the Sunday afternoon automobile races and then back to my home for one of Mother's famous snacks. The table was laden with cheeses, cold cuts, crackers, cookies, and cakes. (I always said that my boyfriends liked my mother better than me.)

On that first date, Ernie and I talked freely. I experienced a feeling of comfort with him that was new to me. He laughed at my jokes and responded with gentleness to my fear of the colliding automobiles during the demolition race.

I found it easy to respond with an excited yes each time he asked for another date. I felt loved and protected when we were together. Life had meaning and purpose.

Ernie helped me study for exams and typed my class notes. His schedule was more flexible than mine, because he was a college sophomore. He picked me up each day after my last class, and we sipped Cokes at the Toot and Tell Drive-in.

All of life centered around one focal point—Ernie.

Decisions about what clothes to buy, what foods to eat, and even where to go to college revolved around my desire to please Ernie.

In the spring of my senior year, we decided to get married. Ernie's basketball coach, Pop Frazier, bypassed Ernie and came straight to me. His words were harsh: "Ginny, if you get married, you will end up having 10 kids and living on welfare. You are too young. Get your education now and think of marriage later!"

While I idolized Pop, I was set upon being Ernie's wife. I visualized us walking together in the rain, sharing our every thought, and blissfully letting the rest of the world go by.

We were married in March, and I loved being Ernie's wife: cooking, cleaning, and soon planning for our baby. But before long, my fairy-tale world was jolted into reality. My nights were sleepless, and I began to question.

Why am I lonely when Ernie is by my side?

What is it that I am missing?

Do I need my own career?

Did I get married too young?

There was a missing link, and I could not put my finger on it. I was physically, emotionally, and mentally strong. So what was it that I lacked? Why this emptiness deep inside?

Because my spiritual side was flat, one of life's punches sent me skidding.

It was a Saturday afternoon in July. We were seated outside the Dairy Queen, eating banana splits, when Ernie looked into my eyes and said, "I don't love you anymore." My entire existence crumbled at my feet.

I didn't say one word, nor did Ernie. We finished eating in silence and walked thoughtfully to our campus apartment. I retreated to the bedroom and closed the door. I cried myself to sleep.

Upon waking, I looked out at the orange and gold

sunset and asked myself, Is this the final sunset for Ernie and me? Is it over? Is there even a ray of hope?

I walked into the living room where Ernie sat reading the newspaper. I rubbed his shoulders gently and whispered, "I still love you." There was no answer.

Any way I viewed the situation, I needed something more. If I were to live alone, I needed help. If I stayed with Ernie and tried to rebuild our marriage, I needed help.

Suddenly I had time for spiritual consideration. Physical, emotional, and mental strength wasn't enough. I needed God. I needed the forgiveness that He provided through His Son, Jesus. I needed the daily strength that only He could give.

I knelt on my knees beside an old gray davenport and prayed, Jesus, forgive me for all the wrong I have done to You, to others, and to myself. Forgive me, and fill me with Your presence." That's all I said. But when I opened my eyes, my entire being was peaceful. I knew I could face tomorrow.

The spots had been washed off the window of my perceptions. Our faults and differences focused into puzzle pieces that had the potential to fit together in unity and harmony. However, the task at hand was not easy, for the pieces were scattered. The laborious challenge was to hunt the missing ones and place them into proper sequence again.

As the weeks unfolded into months, God's love for me enabled me to love Ernie. Eventually his love was likewise rekindled for me.

It was much different from our first date, where communication was natural and acceptance was unrestricted. Lines of affection and mutual respect had been severed. Splicing them back together was tedious and tiresome. However, I was determined, first, to live a vital and healthy life-style myself, and second, to help Ernie reach his potential.

I read books like *Dare to Live Now, Hotline to Heaven, God Calling,* and *My Utmost for His Highest.* I read the Bible daily and entered the world of journaling. I wrote my thoughts, successes, failures, dreams, and hopes. I tried new methods of responding to Ernie and logged them in the journal. I adopted the ones that worked and discarded the rest. One concept that altered my life-style was that when I was unhappy, God usually wanted to change me and not the circumstances.

Little by little I began to change, taking responsibility for my actions and feelings. I quit blaming Ernie when I was unhappy. I also allowed him the freedom to be the person he chose to be. I quit judging him.

Ernie often forgot my birthday. I would get up with a cheery smile and the anticipation that he would pull me close and say, "Happy Birthday." But the morning routine would carry on in the usual manner. By noon I would be hurt, and by evening I would be angry. In accepting responsibility for my feelings, I accepted Ernie's forgetfulness. I quit blaming him. Instead, I started two weeks early to prepare for my birthday. I planned to celebrate instead of becoming angry that he didn't. (On my 50th he surprised me with a birthday party that made up for every one he forgot.)

As my attitude changed, Ernie began to change. The battlefield between us calmed, and communication began to flow.

There are still sleepless nights, but not the same loneliness, for the spiritual side of my personality is as well-rounded as my emotional, physical, and mental sides.

Spiritual maintenance is necessary in order to assure the vitality necessary to roll with life's punches.

Spiritual life without prayer is weak, just as physical life without food is weak. Prayer is simply communicating with God. It should not be misunderstood as lofty or wordy phrases that no one understands or comprehends.

Prayer is telling God that I don't know how to communicate with our teenager and asking Him for the right words to say.

On Roe's 18th birthday he asked, "Mom, now that I am 18, can I live the way I want to and still live at home?" That was a nervy question. I knew that meant alcohol, parties, and late nights.

I silently prayed, "Lord, what do I say? How do I deal with this question? If I say no, he will get angry; and You know, God, how hard it is for me to deal with conflict. If I say yes, I will be violating our values and saying to our younger children that it is OK for them when they turn 18."

My response to Roe was as articulate as if I had been pondering it for weeks rather than only a moment. "Son, I'll pray 10 minutes each day about this decision. You pray 10 minutes daily, and we will talk it over in a week."

That response was insight far beyond me. What could he say except, "OK, Mom." The matter never came up again, and our relationship was not damaged.

Prayer is also taking our financial needs to Him and seeking direction.

Ernie is the money manager at our home; I am the spender. He always knows how much money he has in his wallet, and I don't know if I have $10.00 or $2.00. For me, "Close is good enough." Consequently, we have experienced many conflicts concerning financial matters.

In desperation I prayed, "Lord, I need some freedom concerning personal finances. I trust Ernie to pay the bills and keep us out of the red. But I need some dollars that don't have to be given an exact accounting for where and when they were spent."

This prayer was not answered in an instant. But little by little God has led Ernie and me to an agreement. We budget a set amount of dollars each month that I do not have to give an accounting for. I am finally free. However, I cannot go to Ernie for more when the money is spent; I have to wait until the next pay period. Because of prayer, we arrived at a solution through which we both have freedom.

Prayer is talking to God during the loneliness of midnight hours and being confident He hears.

It was 4 A.M. The sleeping pills hadn't taken effect. The footsteps of nurses and the coughs of patients were a steady reminder that the surgery was scheduled for 7 A.M. In three hours I would be at the mercy of the doctors and the other operating room personnel.

I needed someone to talk to, to express feelings to. After picking up the phone and starting to dial, I didn't finish, for Ernie was certain to be asleep. There were others who could be called; my sister, the pastor, or that special friend would listen. But they, too, would be asleep.

I turned on the light, reached for the journal, and began to write: "Lord, I'm scared. I'm lonely. I need someone to talk to."

On the pages of the journal I prayed to God. He heard and replaced my fears with His peace.

Reading the Bible is the other side of spiritual communication. The Bible is God's Word. Through it He instructs us, teaches us, rebukes us, and trains us in righteousness (right living).

Ernie's words offended me. They seemed accusing and insensitive. Actually, he only asked the question, "What do you weigh?" But to me, who has a weight problem, that was a loaded question.

My mind conjured up several ways to get even: Quit eating and starve; eat everything in sight and really get fat; or just plain tell him to mind his own business.

I opened the Bible and began reading. Shortly the words jumped off the page: "Drop the matter before a dispute breaks out" (Prov. 17:14). I laughed out loud. I was being ridiculous; and in the Bible, which was written 2,000 to 3,500 years ago, was the needed wisdom.

Spiritual well-roundedness requires regular contact with God through prayer, Bible reading, and sharing with others the love, compassion, tenderness, and concern that God has for us.

It's the input/output concept. When we put God's Word into our minds every day but fail to share it with others, it stagnates and becomes useless in keeping us spiritually well-rounded. Also, when we neglect to communicate with Him, we lose the keen edge on our spiritual life.

A friend, Cathy, is teaching school this year after being a homemaker for 10 years. Her life is busy, and she feels she is going in a thousand directions all at once. During Christmas vacation, she also took a vacation from her spiritual expression. The first day she knew it, the second day her family knew it, and the third day a friend who needed help knew it, because Cathy had nothing to give. While she vacationed from her spiritual renewal process, her reservoir dried up. Then, when she needed to give, there was nothing to give. Her friend went away empty.

It takes 1½ hours to groom myself for the day. I exercise, shower, wash and curl my hair, brush my teeth, put on clean clothes, and eat breakfast.

It takes 30 minutes to prepare spiritually for the day. I read the Bible, read a devotional, write requests in the journal, thank God for our family, and pray for my students. Because I leave for work at 8 A.M., the alarm goes off at 5:30 A.M. This leaves a little snooze time.

If we want to roll with life's punches, to remain effective and productive in the midst of them, we must choose to plan into each day some times for spiritual input and output.

SPIRITUAL PLAN

Drill 1: Meditation

Choose a favorite meditation or scripture to meditate on for one week. Read it slowly, aloud in the morning, at noon, and before going to bed.

An example is the Prayer of Serenity:

Lord, grant me the serenity to accept
the things I cannot change,
The courage to change the things I can,
And the wisdom to know the difference.

Drill 2: Respond

Choose a meditation or scripture from the Bible. Read it thoughtfully, and respond to it by asking yourself questions and writing your answers.

The following example is taken from Phil. 4:6-7.

"Do not be anxious about anything, but in everything, by prayer and petition, with thanksgiving, present your requests to God. And the peace of God, which transcends all understanding, will guard your hearts and your minds in Christ Jesus."

The promise is not having our own way, but having peace.

1. What situation or circumstance in my life is causing me to be anxious?

2. If I could have my own way, how would I ask God to solve the situation?

69

3. Is there anything in the situation or circumstance for which I can be thankful?

4. What part of the situation is difficult for me to trust God with?

5. Do I want my way or God's peace?

Drill 3: Prayer

Prayer is communication with God. Prayer is thanking Him for who He is, asking Him questions, and telling Him how we feel or what we think.

A follow-up prayer to Phil. 4:6-7 might be:

Dear Jesus,

     I am anxious about _____.

But on the basis of Your promise of peace (Phil. 4:6-7)

I thank You for _____

and ask You to _____

_____.

And, Jesus, I accept Your gift of peace and promise that You will guard my heart and my mind. Thank You.

Prayer is also seeking guidance and wisdom.

Dear Jesus,

     I have a scheduling conflict today. The insurance man is late for our appointment, and I have to be at a funeral in 30 minutes. Please calm me and work out the details. Thank You.

Prayer changes things. Actually prayer changes me. After praying about a conflict, I can proceed with quietness and confidence.

Drill 4: Evaluation

At the end of the week write a summary of how you were spiritually stimulated through meditation and prayer. Tell how that affected your ability to roll.

_____

_____

_____

_____

_____

_____

_____

_____

_____

_____

"Trust in the Lord with all your heart and lean not on your own understanding; in all your ways acknowledge him, and he will make your paths straight" (Prov. 3:5-6).

7

To Roll Is a Choice

Basketball games are not won by accident. They are won by teams who spend hours in practice and have a game plan.

Well-roundedness doesn't happen by accident; it comes through responsibility. Accepting that responsibility means using all of the resources available to you. You have power to learn, power to change, power to choose.

We are privileged to live in a generation that affords us opportunity to increase our knowledge and to learn new coping skills. When Roe was about 20, his life-style was causing me frustration and stress. I didn't know how to cope and didn't know where to go for help.

Help came through a television program. A psychiatrist led a mother whose son died, through the grieving process. She was forced to relive her son's life by looking at his pictures and sharing the stories each one represented with her therapist. The most difficult and the most healing part of her therapy was when she verbally released her son to death and accepted the fact that he was gone and would not return.

While we had not lost Roe to death, we were losing him to adulthood, to life. He was becoming the person he chose to be and not necessarily what we wanted him to be. However, the skills from the television program were applicable to the loss and grieving.

It was time to put the grief process, as understood from that viewing, into action. First, I pulled the photo albums off the shelf and started reliving Roe's life. Each picture was a story. I laughed at the funny ones and cried over the sad ones. The process was enjoyable until his 16th birthday picture. I couldn't look him in the eye. This picture represented the age he began to pull away from our values and try on new ones for himself.

As I continued to turn the pages of his album, the tears began to flow. I relived all of the hurt, the harsh words, the misunderstandings. I cried as I have never cried before or since.

After closing the album, I was exhausted. The tears had ceased to flow, and my body lay limp across the bed.

"I let you go, son. I let you go now. You may be the adult that you choose to be. You are free." The words spoken were soothing to my spirit and calming to my emotions. I set Roe free and set myself free at the same time.

I leafed back to his 16th birthday picture and looked at him again. Our eyes met. His smile was reassuring. He would become a man to be proud of. I placed his picture on the bed stand, put a cool cloth on my swollen eyes, and whispered, "Thanks, Lord, for the instruction that was so helpful."

It is your responsibility to create your own well-roundedness through effort and knowledge. Right things, persistently done, become pleasurable.

No two people's physical, emotional, mental, or spiritual program will be the same. Only you can sense what works and what doesn't work for you. The more you learn about yourself and your needs, the more sensitive and skilled you become.

It is important to identify our problem areas and to

determine exactly what characteristics should be fused into our life-style.

During my growing-up years I developed the habit of using verbal sarcasm, being quick-witted and sharp-tongued. Whatever the situation or conflict, out came a sarcastic comment.

As an adult, I didn't like this habit and had a strong desire to replace it with a gentle spirit. However, it wasn't until I labeled the problem, and called it by name, that it could be determined what it should be exchanged for.

The desired change was formulated into a statement: "I am sarcastic but want to replace that behavior with a gentle spirit."

After admitting the problem inwardly, I found it necessary to admit to others this sarcastic bent and ask them to help me overcome it.

Most importantly, I had to admit my fault, my sin, to Jesus. I asked Him to forgive me and to remake me into a gentle, soft-spoken person. He did. But I had to take action myself. He provided the power for my action. Slowly I was able to replace sharp words with softer ones.

The clincher came last fall when a friend made a negative comment about my jogging. I opened my mouth, put him in his place, and then left the room. A week later he came and asked if he had offended me.

"Dick," I replied, "I used to be extremely sarcastic and didn't like that characteristic. I have worked hard to overcome it and have prayed for God's help. You are the only one in my world who causes me to resort to my old life-style. We must change the verbal interaction we have."

We are learning to speak to each other in more positive ways. It isn't easy, for our relationship has been a sarcastic one from the beginning. But little by little we are both becoming more comfortable in our new conversation style.

We differ in our weaknesses as well as our strengths. I am a fragile person in many respects. There are definite weaknesses in all areas of my personality. To overcome physical weaknesses, I plan for physical strength, putting specifics into the daily schedule to assure physical stamina.

Recently I attended a faculty breakfast. While viewing the menu, my eyes focused on the cheese omelets, bacon, and hash browns, all favorites. Then came the experience of inner conflict between what I really wanted to eat and what would give my body strength and energy until noon.

No one goes out to breakfast and orders oatmeal and whole wheat toast without butter. And I was reluctant to do so for fear of what my colleagues would think.

Then I remembered the 32 students I was responsible to teach that day. Eating all the favorites on the menu would make me less than my best for them; by 10:30 I would be sluggish and drowsy.

So the order was made for oatmeal and whole wheat toast. By doing so, I planned for physical stamina. And because of planning for proper nutrition and making proper choices, I enjoyed physical strength instead of weakness.

In much the same way, I plan emotional stability into the day. I have assessed my emotional makeup and identified my weaknesses.

None of us feel good about ourselves when we procrastinate. Procrastination causes emotional weakness. It also causes weaknesses in relationships because we are forced to make excuses for incomplete tasks.

I have begun to make use of little nuggets of time. Large amounts of time are rare in the schedule, and waiting for them means putting off responsibilities. This neglect causes me to be emotionally weak.

For example, we may be having company for dinner next Friday evening. I also have to teach school Monday through Friday. There are no large segments of time to prepare the meal. I could wait until Friday afternoon, stop at the store, rush home, prepare a pan of lasagna, cut up the salad, set the table, send our daughter, Maaike, out to buy a pie, and be an emotional wreck when the guests arrive.

However, instead of waiting until Friday, I will do the shopping Monday after school, make a frozen dessert Tuesday evening, prepare and freeze the lasagna Wednesday after school, vacuum the floor and set the table Thursday evening. Then on Friday, I will come home, cut up the salad, put the lasagna in the microwave, take a shower and have emotional confidence when our guests arrive.

Proper planning and efficient use of small bits of time strengthen our emotional state.

My mental outlook is strengthened by taking time daily to meditate and reflect on the current situation and develop a plan by which I can proceed with peace of mind. I desire to live a single-minded life whereby I face each situation with confidence, poise, and adequacy. I desire this so intently that I plan moments to ponder the important versus the urgent.

The important things in life are those of lasting value. The urgent are the ones that are screaming for attention *now* but will not matter 10 years from now.

Today is a prime example of the mental conflict between the important and the urgent. It is difficult for me to understand the importance of sitting here writing this book. There is no immediate reinforcement for doing it. I also have no absolute assurance it will ever be published or that it will ever help another person.

However, in taking time to clear my mind this morning and to consider the day's activities, I had a deep inner awareness that the writing is the important and the dust on the furniture is the urgent.

Therefore I chose the important and am proceeding with the desired peace of mind. The furniture will get dusted and the other urgent needs will be met because my productivity and efficiency levels are significantly higher when I have singleness of mind.

Most importantly, I plan for spiritual strength. I cannot expect God to automatically zap me with spiritual fortitude for the day. I must exercise spiritual muscles as well as physical muscles if I expect to be strong.

Two weeks ago Carolyn and I ate our lunch in the car. Carolyn was a new acquaintance, and we were visiting about the difficult and hurtful situations in her life. As we talked, it became apparent that she needed spiritual strength. She would not be able to combat her circumstances on physical, emotional, and mental strength. She needed to add the fourth dimension to her coping skills.

Carolyn had never heard before that through Jesus she could have the power of God at work in her life on a moment-by-moment basis. Since the concept was new to her, she chose to think about it for a couple of days and decide for herself whether or not she wanted to invite Jesus into her life.

On Friday of that week, Carolyn said, "I have thought about it, and I am ready." She prayed a simple prayer inviting Jesus to come into her life. She asked Him to forgive her of her sins and thanked Him for doing so.

In order for Carolyn to grow and be strengthened spiritually, she now has to choose to develop as a new spiritual person.

First, she memorized two verses from the Bible that assured her of her new life in Christ. They are found in 1 John 5:11-12: "And this is the testimony: God has given us eternal life, and this life is in his Son. He who has the Son has life; he who does not have the Son of God does not have life."

Second, she purchased a journal and began writing her prayers each day. She has discovered that as she writes her need as a prayer to God, her spirit is strengthened. She also now realizes that when God answers her prayers, her spiritual strength is even greater.

Carolyn had an appointment with her divorce mediator and her husband. Before she went, she prayed, "Lord, give me confidence and poise as I state my needs, and take away the power struggle that is so intense."

The next time we met, Carolyn's smile evidenced the fact that God had answered her prayer. She said, "Ginny, I couldn't believe it. I was so calm and poised. And after the meeting with the mediator, my husband took me to coffee. We actually discussed our needs without any power struggle." That is spiritual strength! And it was available to Carolyn because she put spiritual activities into her life and into her day.

In order to assess your strengths and your weaknesses, learn as much about yourself as possible. First, observe your thoughts, feelings, and desires. Second, read books and magazine articles that deal with your set of strengths and weaknesses.

Third, talk to others and listen to them. Use all available resources. When I meet someone who seems to be coping better with life, I find ways to be in their company in order to glean from the insights they possess.

Fourth, believe in discipline, but be patient with yourself. And don't give up too soon.

For years I inwardly, if not outwardly, rebelled at the word *discipline.* I believed that to be disciplined was to become bound, to give up all freedom. I have since learned that discipline in body, mind, and spirit provides the greatest freedom of all.

At this writing I am 50, and due to living a disciplined life-style, I enjoy freedoms that could not be enjoyed otherwise. Physically, I can climb a mountain, go on bike hikes with my fourth graders, and run 13 miles without stopping. In fact, I can do most anything I choose.

I cope with midlife's emotional changes without bouts of depression or mood-changing chemicals. I continue to challenge my mind by thinking new thoughts and formulating ideas and opinions. And I am free in my spirit.

No, I am not wonderful all of the time! But when there are problems, there are also ways to come back to the abundant life-style.

This morning when getting up, I was an absolute mess! I felt awful, looked awful, and acted awful. But soon I got tired of being awful. I ate breakfast, did a few jumping jacks, showered, spent some time meditating, and before long, felt great.

Without the disciplines, I would still be feeling awful.

Ensuring well-roundedness, that ability to roll with life's punches, takes 40 minutes daily. You can increase your efficiency and productivity levels within a two-week period.

Have a game plan. Put the following ingredients into your daily schedule and be prepared to roll instead of skid.

A. *PHYSICAL WELL-ROUNDEDNESS*
  1. Take a brisk walk at a comfortable pace to replenish your body with fresh oxygen.
  2. Provide yourself with the sleep that your body requires (usually 6-8 hours).
  3. Drink 8 glasses of water.
  4. Include in your diet 2 fruits, 2 vegetables, 8 oz. protein, 2 bread servings, and one milk serving.
  5. Eat or drink nothing after 8 P.M.

B. *EMOTIONAL WELL-ROUNDEDNESS*
  1. Choose one small task and complete it within a 10-minute span.

2. Do your best in everything you do.
3. Say no to responsibilities that will overload you.
4. Nurture relationships; take a minute to write a note or make a phone call to say, "I care."

C. *MENTAL WELL-ROUNDEDNESS*
1. Read books and articles that stimulate thought patterns.
2. Think positive thoughts. "Whatsoever things are honest, . . . whatsoever things are pure, whatsoever things are lovely, . . . think on these things" (Phil. 4:8, KJV).
3. Guard your mind from negative books, articles, movies, and conversations.

D. *SPIRITUAL WELL-ROUNDEDNESS*
1. Read God's Word, the Bible.
Read one portion of Scripture until it is part of you. Meditate on it.
2. Pray. Don't be anxious about anything; tell God your needs.
3. Talk freely with others about your faith.

Lest you conclude that I am not in tune with the real world and the forces that fight against us, here is a recounting of a recent day.

Despair escaped from my lips in words and feelings that I didn't even know were stored in my memory bank.

I was physically exhausted, emotionally drained, mentally agitated, and spiritually flat when one of life's punches hit: Ernie broke his leg playing softball. Now that doesn't sound like much, but his broken leg meant that the summer I had planned for leisure, reading, and tennis lessons would be spent being a nurse, mowing the lawn, and teaching his summer school class at the college.

Notice, will you, the large amount of selfishness that permeated my mind-set. Leisure, reading, and tennis lessons were all for *my* pleasure, ease, and profit. Never mind the pain, discomfort, inconvenience, and recuperation my husband would have to suffer, as well as his having to miss far more fun things than I would that summer.

But all this meant nothing to me. I literally flew into a rage.

"It is all in vain! I have given so much, and I am so empty! Why, God, have You forsaken me? I have given my life for You, for others, and for the work of Your kingdom. Is it all a lie? Is there anything to this life-style that I proclaim and live?"

Embarrassed and defeated, I retreated to the bedroom to sob. Ernie came and prayed that I would know peace, God's peace. As he prayed, I relaxed and fell asleep.

Upon waking, I began reading the Bible. I had to confess to God the rash statements and questions uttered earlier. He knows that I will follow Him until the end of time. He also knew that the trials of life had overloaded me in recent days.

Robert had dropped out of college in the middle of the term.

Maaike had another allergy attack. This one could have taken her life.

So as I lay on the bed, reading the Bible, the Holy Spirit reminded me that even Jesus cried out, "My God, my God, why hast thou forsaken me?" (Matt. 27:46; Mark 15:34, both KJV).

What relief! What assurance! What comfort! He was "in all points tempted like as we are, yet without sin" (Heb. 4:15, KJV). His life among us gives Him sympathy when we struggle; His perfect example causes us to confess when we fail.

I have courage once more. God has regenerated my capacity to roll.

Taking a close look at that past week, however, I noticed that I had been too busy to exercise, had not had the needed sleep, and had rushed meditation times. What would have been the reaction to Ernie's broken leg if I had been well-rounded? What if busyness had not robbed me of sleep, exercise, and the daily quiet time? It is very possible I would have been able to roll with it.

Tonight I made a new start, with new determination. When I am passed, dribbled, or shot through the hoop of life's situations, I must roll! I must succeed in using my body, mind, and spirit to glorify God, by rolling with life's punches.

HELPING OTHERS ROLL

If you are better equipped to roll with life's punches now that you have read and applied these concepts, give this book to a friend who is skidding. Allow the principles to roll on from one generation to another.

"For God did not give us a spirit of timidity, but a spirit of power, of love and of self-discipline" (2 Tim. 1:7).

"Always be prepared to give an answer to everyone who asks you to give the reason for the hope that you have" (1 Pet. 3:15).